To avoid charges items must be returned or
renewed on or before closing time on the last
date marked above.

Items may be renewed unless requested by
another customer, in person or by telephone,
on two occasions only. Your membership card
number will be required.

Please look after this item – you may be
charged for any damage.

Public Record Office
Pocket Guides to Family History

Getting Started in Family History

Using Birth, Marriage and Death Records

Using Census Returns

Using Wills

Using Army Records

Using Navy Records

Tracing Irish Ancestors

Tracing Scottish Ancestors

Using Poor Law Records

Tracing Catholic Ancestors

Tracing Nonconformist Ancestors

Using Medal Records (forthcoming)

Using Criminal Records

USING

CRIMINAL RECORDS

Ruth Paley

Public Record Office
Richmond
Surrey
TW9 4DU

ISBN 1 903365 27 9

A catalogue card for this book is available
from the British Library

Front cover: P Turner and G Kirby, 1871, from
Habitual Criminals Register (PCOM 2/430)

Printed by Cromwell Press, Trowbridge, Wiltshire

CONTENTS

INTRODUCTION

Many families have a criminal or two among their ancestors –
although these are often consigned to oblivion or conveniently
forgotten until someone begins to delve into the family's past.
As soon as their existence has been discovered, it is natural to
want to know more about them. With what crime or crimes
were they charged? What happened to them? Were they in
fact guilty? And if so, how did they become involved in crime?

This Pocket Guide will help you trace criminal cases in
England and Wales from about 1540 to the middle of the 20th
century. Within that period it attempts to be reasonably
comprehensive, covering records of investigation, trial and
punishment held at the Public Record Office or by local record
offices. It does not cover the records of medieval eyres or
prosecutions in manorial or church courts.

When you succeed in finding a record of the charges against
your ancestor giving parish of residence, occupation and
details of his or her crime, you will no doubt be delighted, but
a word of warning: as you will discover from the section on
trial records, such information is rarely accurate before 1916
and can be positively misleading. It should also be pointed
that it may take time to identify or locate all the relevant
material, since the progress of a criminal through the legal
system generated a mass of documentation. Nevertheless, it
is worth persevering. Both the search itself and the results
may prove to be truly fascinating.

CAN'T WAIT TO GET STARTED?

Then don't wait! There is no right or wrong way of conducting this kind of research. Much depends on what you already know. This guide is written in a logical sequence; it starts with the commission of a crime then moves to trial, conviction and punishment, but the information you have is unlikely to fit the sequence quite so neatly. You may know little more than that you have an ancestor who was a prisoner on census night, or that he or she was transported. You may have information from a newspaper account or from Poor Law records. You may have no more than a shadowy piece of family folklore.

For a quick start, dip in wherever seems most appropriate. If your hard information is about imprisonment or transportation, then read those sections first, but be prepared to read the guide through carefully later; it will help you to make sense of what you find, and it will also open up possibilities for additional research.

FIRST STEPS

Assemble all the information you have. Ideally you need to know the place and date of trial and something about the sentence. If you don't have this information, re-examine your evidence in the light of the advice and explanations given in this guide. To know when and where someone was hanged or was in gaol, or to know within a few years the date of a convict's arrival in a prison colony, is to know enough to narrow the search. If you have none of this information, then your search will be far more difficult and time-consuming.

Think carefully about what it is that you want to find out. Almost everyone who starts out researching criminal ancestors begins by looking for trial records – and they are almost always disappointed, because trial records in England and Wales are singularly uninformative. The trial records do not normally contain any transcripts of evidence and, as mentioned in the Introduction, they can be extremely misleading. If you are looking for details of evidence given in court, then you may well be better advised to look for a newspaper or pamphlet account of the trial. If what you want

---

Reading old legal documents

Except for a brief period in the 1650s, trial records before 1733 are written in heavily abbreviated Latin and in distinctive legal scripts. To decipher them effectively, some knowledge of Latin and palaeography is needed. For a selection of books on old handwriting and on Latin that may be of help if your research stretches back beyond 1733, see p. 60.

to know is something about your ancestor's family, working life or place of birth, then you would be better off looking for an application for mercy.

In order to use criminal records effectively, you need to learn something about the structure and processes of the criminal justice system. A search for criminal ancestors can be complex – but you can save time and effort by targeting your search as accurately as possible.

PUBLISHED WORKS AND INDEXES

The easiest way to trace a trial is through a published work
(for details of useful publications, see p. 61). 'True crime'
magazines are not a modern invention: from at least the 17th
century, publishers have been keen to cash in on our eternal
fascination with the seamier side of life. Perhaps the best
known is the series covering trials at the Old Bailey. This
series started in the 1680s – but the Guildhall Library in
London is one of the few places that have such early copies.
Those that were published between 1714 and 1834 are
available on microfilm; there are copies at the Public Record
Office in the record series PCOM 1 (1801–1904) and CRIM 10
(1834–1912). Many published accounts of trials have been
brought together and published on microfilm as *British Trials*
(a copy is available at the PRO).

A close reading of a published account will not only tell you
about what happened in court, it will almost certainly tell you
which court it was. A speculative search through newspapers
may seem a daunting prospect, but remember that local record
offices and local-studies libraries have often compiled their
own indexes to local newspapers. *The Times* is held at most
reference libraries, including the PRO library, on microfilm. It
is indexed, and CD-ROM copies of the indexes are available in
the PRO library. In general, local newspapers for areas well
away from London were first published in the mid 18th
century, while those for London did not start until the later
part of the 19th century. You can find out about locations and
survival from the Gibson guide, *Local Newspapers*. Pamphlets
may be more difficult to find. Those published before 1800 are
listed in the *English Short Title Catalogue* which, like *The
Times,* is available at good central reference libraries; ask your
librarian for advice on how to consult it.

There are a variety of indexes that might help. For those who were transported to America, you should start with Coldham's indexes to migrants to America. The indexes to criminal petitions will help identify those transported to Australia, as will the index to the *New South Wales Convict Indents and Ships*, which records the names and aliases of the convicts who arrived in New South Wales and Van Diemen's Land 1788–1842 and the ships on which they arrived, together with the various published early censuses of Australia. Copies of all of these are available in the PRO library. For the 16th to 18th centuries, you should also look at the indexes to the published *Calendars of State Papers* (both domestic and colonial) and *Calendar of Home Office Papers*; the *Calendar of State Papers Colonial* has also been published on CD-ROM.

Those who were tried in the 16th and 17th centuries at assizes in the Home Counties are indexed in the *Calendar of Assize Records*. Knafla's *Kent at Law* indexes all those tried in Kent in 1602. For the 19th century there are original indexes to prisoners transferred from one prison to another, 1843–71, in PRO series PCOM 6. There are some specialist indexes to petitions for mercy and the criminal registers 1805–92 by Chambers and Tamblin.

Some indexes are available via the internet, so it is worth exploring the links available on major family history sites such as GENUKI and Cyndi's List (see p. 46). The PRO catalogue sometimes lists names of defendants, so an on-line search specifying the department as ASSI, HO or TS might be useful. Some local record offices also have catalogues that list defendants; and an increasing number of their catalogues are available through A2A (the Access to Archives project), which you can access from the PRO website (see p. 47).

COMMITTING THE CRIME

Not all illegal or immoral acts are crimes. Crimes are defined by the law and are subject to shifting definitions, as new laws are enacted and old ones repealed or remodelled. Until 1967, crimes were either felonies or misdemeanours. The distinction was procedurally important. Felonies were not necessarily more serious than misdemeanours (although most serious crimes – murder, arson, rape, robbery – were felonies) but they had to be tried by jury. The value of the stolen goods was often important in distinguishing between offences: a pickpocket committed a felony if he or she stole goods worth more than a shilling (12 old pence, or 5p in decimal coinage). But there could be other factors: highway robbery was a felony irrespective of the amount stolen – but only if the victim was 'put in fear'.

Understanding the technicalities about definitions of crimes may seem to be somewhat esoteric, but it is often useful. It can help you to identify the most likely court of trial and also to understand the annotations on trial documents. Use a good legal manual or law dictionary and, because the law changed so often, consult the edition that was published as close as possible to the date of the offence you are trying to trace. Specialist legal manuals on the criminal law were increasingly published from the mid 18th century. The PRO library holds copies of some of the most useful works.

INVESTIGATION AND PROSECUTION

The first modern police force (the Metropolitan Police) was set up in 1829. Before that date, it was up to victims to investigate crimes and organize the prosecution of offenders. There were several options: some people really did investigate matters themselves; others used their servants, the local constable or a thieftaker (a rather dubious sort of private detective, often with strong gangland connections). When it came to the actual prosecution, they might employ a lawyer but unless the case was particularly complicated this was not really necessary, since advice would be readily available from the clerks employed at the court. Not surprisingly, victims were sometimes unable or unwilling to investigate or to pay for a prosecution. They might therefore decide not to prosecute at all, or might decide to prosecute on a lesser charge in order to get things over and done with more quickly and cheaply.

On the other hand, the offence might be so outrageous that friends and neighbours wished to contribute towards the cost, either as individuals or collectively through the vestry. Sometimes local residents clubbed together to form self-help organizations to help with prosecutions. In some particularly serious cases – especially murder, where the victim was of course unable to act – the government might itself pay for the prosecution. Sometimes the government became involved in organizing the prosecution case; but even if government involvement was peripheral, ministers might call for reports about the progress of the investigation.

Even before the foundation of modern police forces, the Home Office occasionally sent London magistrates or their servants ('runners') to investigate provincial crimes. From the mid 19th century all areas had their own police forces, but the high reputation of the Metropolitan Police meant that they were often called in to assist provincial forces – especially in murder cases. The new police forces began to take over the role of organizing prosecutions (aided after 1879 by the Director of Public Prosecutions) and it is generally assumed that by the end of the century almost all prosecutions were brought and paid for by the police.

RECORDS OF INVESTIGATION AND PROSECUTION

This complex situation means that information about the progress of investigations is likely to be found scattered through a variety of sources. The surviving private papers of individuals and solicitors involved in a case are most likely to be in the relevant local record office, which is also the place to look for parish records and the papers of local prosecution societies.

At the PRO it is worth investigating the correspondence of the secretaries of state. Much of their early correspondence is published (and indexed). For 1547–1704, these are known as the *Calendar of State Papers Domestic*. Similar records, 1760–72, are published as the *Calendar of Home Office Papers*. For the period 1705–59, you will need to use the PRO series SP 34, SP 35 and SP 36. From 1773 to 1782, use SP 37 – which continues after 1782 as HO 42. You may be able to consult microfilm copies at one of the Church of Latter-day Saints (LDS) Family History Centres (listed on the Genealogical Society of Utah's website, see p. 46) or at a major reference library or a university library.

After 1841, the main series of correspondence is HO 45; and from 1879 there is supplementary material in HO 144. The papers in HO 144 are those that were originally subject to closure dates longer than normal. Their closed status is reviewed on demand – so if the papers you wish to see are marked 'closed', ask PRO staff for advice.

In addition to its main series of general correspondence, the Home Office developed some specialized file series, which may be useful but will be time-consuming to search effectively. Perhaps the three most useful ones are: HO 44,

Correspondence, George IV and later (1820–61); HO 52, Counties correspondence (1820–50); and HO 40, Correspondence about disturbances (1812–55). Information about offering rewards and pardons to informants is in HO 64 (1820–40), supplemented by HO 75.

Records of police forces are held in local record offices or police museums or by the relevant police force itself. The only exception is the Metropolitan Police Force, which is under the direct control of the Home Office and whose records are therefore held at the PRO (the series most likely to be helpful is MEPO 3). Copies of the *Hue and Cry* and the *Police Gazette* (1828–45), which contain an assortment of interesting details about crime and criminals, are in HO 75.

Case papers of the Director of Public Prosecutions (1889–1983) are in DPP 1 and DPP 2, with registers of cases (1884–1956) in DPP 3.

ⓘ Remember

You can consult copies of the catalogues of local record offices before you visit. Copies of their catalogues are held at the Historical Manuscripts Commission in London, and some can be consulted via the internet by using A2A (the Access to Archives project) on the PRO website.

WHICH COURT?

Several kinds of court could try criminal cases. Starting at the bottom and working upwards, the various courts were:

- A single magistrate sitting in summary jurisdiction (no jury)

- Two or more magistrates sitting as a petty sessions in summary jurisdiction (no jury)

- The body of county or borough magistrates sitting together as general or quarter sessions (jury trial)

- The assizes (jury trial)

- The King's Bench (Crown Side) (jury trial)

The prosecutor's choice was constrained by several factors, not least of which were the following.

Money

In general, the cost of a prosecution became more expensive the further one moved up the hierarchy. A prosecutor who wanted the cheapest option was therefore more likely to opt for the lower courts. Sometimes the prosecutor deliberately chose a more expensive court in order to force the defendant into greater expense.

Distance and timing

The existence of a court of summary jurisdiction (usually known as a petty sessions or magistrates' court) depended on the willingness of the local magistrates to hold one. Until the 1830s there were no rules about the area covered by individual magistrates' courts or about the frequency or times of sittings. Prosecutors might find it much more convenient to go to a higher court, which would be more centrally located and whose times of sitting would be well known. From the 19th century, sittings of magistrates' courts became more organized and this, coupled with the increasing scope of cases they could hear, meant that most minor crimes were tried in magistrates' courts.

Quarter sessions were meetings of the county magistrates held (as the name implies) once a quarter. In some areas additional or general sessions were also held. Assize courts were held twice a year, in the spring and summer. The time of year might therefore become an important factor in the prosecutor's calculations. Was he/she prepared to wait a long time for the next visit of the assize judges? Would he/she be able to get witnesses together at the right time? Did he/she want to be as speedy as possible? Or did he/she want to hold the threat of prosecution over a defendant's head for as long as possible?

Jurisdictional competence

'Jurisdictional competence' is legal jargon for the technicalities that decided which courts could hear different kinds of case. Some offences, especially minor ones, could be prosecuted at any level of the hierarchy; but in general, the more serious the offence the higher the court was likely to be. In most parts of England and Wales, offences that required jury trial would go either to quarter sessions or to the assizes. The magistrates in quarter sessions acted under a commission of the peace. Assize courts were held by visiting judges who acted under commissions of oyer and terminer (meaning 'to hear and judge') and gaol delivery.

In considering jurisdictional competence, remember that changing legal definitions could affect the court of trial. If an act of parliament converted an offence from a misdemeanour into a felony, or vice versa, this would also affect the prosecutor's choice of courts. Since the early 18th century, an increasing number of offences have been removed from jury trial so that they can be dealt with more quickly (and more cheaply) at a magistrates' court. This is another area in which getting to grips with legal technicalities about the definitions of crimes can be vital to the success of your search.

TRIAL RECORDS:
SUMMARY JURISDICTION

Records of individual justices sitting alone rarely survive. If you are interested in finding out more about their powers and activities, see Paley, *Justice in Eighteenth-century Hackney*.

Surviving petty sessions records are most likely to be in the relevant local record office. Records from the early 20th century have survived well; and some counties have good survivals for the 19th century too, but unfortunately they are rarely indexed. Where they do survive they may include registers of summons issued, with brief annotations of resulting process, and perhaps order books and/or minutes of the hearings. Minute books can be extremely informative although, as they were often written during the hearing, they can be difficult to read. If there are no minute books, look for books of orders and summons; the entries may be sparse, but they are still interesting.

(i) **Remember**

If there are no records, or if you are uncertain of the date or location of the trial, remember that local newspapers often give very full accounts of hearings. Trace them through Gibson, *Local Newspapers*.

TRIAL RECORDS: QUARTER SESSIONS AND ASSIZES

What do they contain?

Quarter sessions and assize records are very similar. Early trial records were kept together in rolled files (normally there was a single file for each session). Although usually called indictment files, these often contain a variety of documents, such as recognizances, witness statements, notes about process, jury lists and gaol calendars (lists of prisoners to be tried), all rolled up together. Except in very rare cases, they will *not* include transcripts of evidence. Separate series of records may survive for depositions, process books, entry books and probation or medical reports. Trial records are normally closed for 30 years, but some – especially those involving issues of privacy and confidentiality, such as assaults on children or rape – are closed for longer periods.

What is an indictment and what will it tell me?

Indictments give details of the charge against the defendant. Before 1916 they followed a format that had changed little since the 16th century, except that before 1733 (apart from a brief period during the 1650s) they were in Latin and in distinctive legal scripts. They are written on pieces of parchment of varying sizes and begin with the phrase 'The jurors for our lord the king (or, our lady the queen) present that'; they then give the name of the accused with what appears to be his/her residence and occupation and an account of the alleged crime. But you cannot accept this information at face value – it was concocted for legal purposes not for accuracy! The place of 'residence' is usually the location of the crime, and the 'occupation' is almost invariably given as 'labourer'. To find more reliable information, you need to find a recognizance – usually a long thin strip of parchment. Recognizances record the true names, addresses and occupations of the accused and those who were willing to stand bail for him or her. If there is no recognizance, you may be able to piece the same information together from the depositions, or perhaps from a gaol calendar.

Until the early 20th century, committal proceedings were held before a grand jury. Indictments that went to trial have the words *'true bill'* or *'billa vera'* written on the back. You may also find indictments for cases that never went to trial because the grand jury did not think the prosecution evidence was strong enough: these have *'ign.'* or *'ignoramus'* written on the back. The names of the prosecution witnesses who testified at the committal proceedings are also on the back of the indictment.

As already mentioned, before 1916 indictments used an assortment of convoluted stock phrases developed for legal purposes. All indictments for assault, however minor, describe the victim as being so badly injured 'that his life was despaired of'. The valuations given for stolen goods have more to do with the legal requirements of the charge than the realities of the market place. Offences against statute law are distinguished from those against common law by the words 'against the form of the statute' – although the indictment will rarely tell you *which* statute, let alone which section of it. If you really want to understand what the charge was, then you will need to consult a legal manual, preferably one published as close to the date of the trial as possible.

The outcome of the trial is noted on the indictment, usually just above the name of the accused. The notes are always in Latin until 1733, and are still mostly in Latin even long afterwards. Commonly used phrases and abbreviations include:

billa vera there is a case to answer
ca null (catalla nulla) no goods/chattels to forfeit
cog ind (cognovit indictamentum) confessed
cul (culpabilis) guilty
ign (ignoramus) no case to answer
non cul nec re (non culpabilis nec retraxit) not guilty and did not flee
po se (ponit se super patriam) pleads not guilty
sus (suspendatur) sentenced to hang

After 1916, indictments set out the charge(s) against the accused very clearly, and you will have no difficulty working out just what the defendant was supposed to have done.

What about other trial records?

Depositions can be extremely informative, but their survival tends to be poor. In addition to the normal hazards of time, assize depositions of the 19th and early 20th centuries have been subjected to systematic and unsympathetic weeding, only those taken in cases of 'serious' crime (treason, sedition, murder, riot) being retained. On the plus side, the survivals might include items produced in evidence at the trial, such as letters, maps and photographs. Be warned: in some cases this material can be highly distressing.

If you are conducting a speculative search over several years or there are no surviving indictment or deposition files, look for notes about the management of the caseload. These are kept in volumes variously known as crown minute books, court books or gaol books. They usually contain lists of cases, often with summaries of verdict and sentence.

As indicated above, transcripts of evidence do not form part of the trial record. The best place to find out what was said in court is in a newspaper report. However, there are some transcripts in the PRO. Some of these were preserved as part of campaigns for mercy (see p. 41); others (selected trials only, 1846–1931) are in DPP 4.

Quarter sessions records are held at local record offices: use Gibson, *Quarter Sessions*, to trace them. Many quarter sessions records have been transcribed or calendared by local record societies. You can find out about local record society publications by using Mullins, *Texts and Calendars*. Use the website of the Historical Manuscripts Commission to find out about similar works published since 1982.

Where can I find assize trial records?

Records of trials at assizes are held in the ASSI series at the PRO. Use the tables on pp. 50–59 to find the records that survive for your county.

Where are Welsh records before 1830?

In Wales the functions of the assizes were carried out by the court of Great Sessions until its abolition in 1830; these records are now in the National Library of Wales. To find out more, consult Parry, *Guide to the Records of the Great Sessions*.

What about London before 1834?

The City of London was (and still is) a specific administrative area at the heart of the modern metropolitan area. The urban sprawl around it was in the county of Middlesex until 1888, when it was combined with parts of Essex, Surrey and Kent to form the new county of London. Until 1834, neither London nor Middlesex had assize courts in the usual way. They shared a county gaol (Newgate), and serious crimes were tried at the Old Bailey. Some crimes that in other counties would have been tried at assizes courts were tried at the Middlesex sessions, whose records are held by the London Metropolitan Archives.

Records of trials at the Old Bailey before 1834 are split: the London cases are held by the Corporation of London Record Office, whereas the Middlesex cases are at the London Metropolitan Archives. So to trace the records of an Old Bailey trial before 1834, you need to know whether it was a London or a Middlesex case. The printed Old Bailey Sessions

Papers indicate whether a case was tried by the Middlesex or the London jury. Although indictment files survive for both jurisdictions, the survival of other papers (especially depositions and witness statements) is poor.

After 1834 the situation is much simpler. The old court at the Old Bailey was replaced by the new Central Criminal Court. The Central Criminal Court had the same powers as an assize court. It heard cases from Middlesex and London as before, but added the urban fringes of Surrey, Kent and Essex to its jurisdiction. Only a 2 per cent sample of the depositions and associated trial papers survive: they are held at the PRO. Since the Central Criminal Court is still commonly referred to as the Old Bailey, make sure you check the date of trial – or you could end up at the wrong record office!

TRIALS IN THE KING'S BENCH
(CROWN SIDE)

The King's Bench (or Queen's Bench, as appropriate) was the highest court of common law in England and Wales. It divided its business into two categories. Criminal cases were tried on the Crown Side. Cases that would now be classed as civil actions were heard on the Plea Side and are not covered in this guide.

If you think your case was tried by the King's Bench, then start with the indexes to defendants. These are not entirely reliable but are still useful. They are alphabetical by first letter of surname, then chronological by term and year. The number to the left of the surname identifies the indictment or information on the relevant indictment file.

King's Bench – indexes of defendants		
1673–1843	London and Middlesex	IND 1/6669–6677
1638–1704, 1765–1843	All counties except London and Middlesex	IND 1/6680–6684
1682–99	London, Middlesex and some defendants in northern counties	IND 1/6678–6679

For 1844–59 there is a modern card index to the plea rolls (KB 28), giving the names of prosecutors and defendants, but only for those cases where a formal judgement was entered.

No index? Or defendant's name not indexed?

You will need a rough idea of the date of the case. Go to the first section of the relevant term entries on the controlment rolls (KB 29): this lists all the cases for the term with the jurisdiction and indictment number. For 1844–98, try the modern pye books (IND 1/6685–6686, IND 1/6687/1–2). Like the controlment rolls, these are chronological – but they give more information (names of defendants, attorneys, jurisdiction and a summary of proceedings). Remember that some of these cases were only attempted prosecutions and never actually came to trial. If the judges disallowed the prosecution, then there will be nothing in the indictment files, although it may still be worth searching for depositions. Use the indexes to depositions (KB 39) to find them.

Where are the indictment files?

King's Bench – indictment files		
Before 1675	All counties	KB 9
1675–1843	London and Middlesex only	KB 10
1675–1843	All counties except London and Middlesex	KB 11
After 1844	All counties	KB 12

The indictment files contain indictments and informations. Informations were charges made directly to the court on the authority of the Master of the court or the Attorney General; they start with the words 'Be it remembered that . . .'. Indictments in the King's Bench do not contain annotations about the outcome of the case.

How do I find out what happened?

Go to the second section of the term's entries on the controlment rolls (KB 29) and work forward until you find an entry for your case (though of course there might not be one!). The notes above the entry record all the proceedings. For London and Middlesex cases 1737–1820, it is easier to use the process books in KB 15/22–29; but these are not as reliable as KB 39. The great docket books (IND 1/6657–6658, IND 1/6652/6–8) were records kept by the clerks to help them keep track of what was going on. They list all steps in process, such as entries of pleas and writs, and often give direct references to the controlment rolls and indictment files; however, they are difficult to use, as entries are grouped by date rather than by case.

The annotations will tell you which terms you should search for depositions (KB 1 and KB 2), rule books (KB 21) and draft rule books (KB 36). There are also contemporary indexes to depositions in KB 39. The depositions are often full and informative.

Treason and sedition

Check the catalogue for the Baga de Secretis (KB 8); this contains information relating to the prosecution case in trials that were of particular concern to the state. Also, look at the published accounts of such trials in Howell's *State Trials* (now available from Jutastat on CD-ROM).

IMPRISONMENT

Today we almost automatically associate punishment with imprisonment. It was not so in the past. The choice of punishments was limited; until the late 17th century, with a single exception, those convicted of treason or a felony faced only one sentence – death. The exception was petty larceny, which could be punished by whipping. Those convicted of misdemeanours were fined or whipped.

Gaols were for remand prisoners and debtors. It was only when people began to believe in the reforming power of imprisonment that it became acceptable to use imprisonment as a punishment in its own right. From time to time, various local initiatives created prisons that were meant to reform their inmates – but these attempts tended to be short-lived, and the new prisons usually ended up much the same as others. The first attempt to impose some uniformity came with the Gaol Act of 1823; inspectors of prisons were appointed in 1835; and further controls were introduced in 1844. The first national convict prisons for adults were Millbank (1816) and Pentonville (1842), both under the direct control of the Home Office. In 1877 prison administration was centralized under a new organization, the Prison Commission.

Until the mid 19th century, then, prisoners would almost certainly be held in a local gaol. So if you know the location of the prison, you are half way to finding the court of trial; and if you know the kind of prison it was, you have narrowed the search still further. A county might have many prisons, but only one would be designated the county gaol – and this was the gaol that was 'delivered' by the assize judges. Other prisons that were set up as reformatories were often called Bridewells, or Houses of Correction. Their inmates were normally tried at quarter sessions. Some were not tried at all, but were sent there for just a few nights – for what we might now term a 'short, sharp shock'.

The development of a centrally controlled national network of prisons enabled some to be developed as specialist reformatories, such as those reserved for the imprisonment of young people or women. But bear in mind that the specialist role of the prison may have changed over the years; although Parkhurst on the Isle of Wight is currently a prison for adult male offenders, it was purpose built, in 1839, for juveniles. Obviously in a system of this kind it is no longer possible to assume that the location of a prisoner bears any relationship to the place of his or her trial. Fortunately, it generated a lot of paperwork, much of which still survives at the PRO.

PRISON RECORDS

How can I trace a prisoner?

Before the 19th century it can be difficult to trace prisoners. Remember that calendars of prisoners often survive in indictment files, as well as in a separate series of their own, and be prepared to check both. Calendars of prisoners are also held in local record offices. For assize prisoners, try sheriffs' vouchers (1758–1832), held at the PRO in E 370/35–51. Since these are expense claims for looking after assize prisoners, they do not include prisoners at quarter sessions. They give sentences, details of time spent in prison and, of course, costs.

By the end of the 18th century, the government had started to keep systematic lists of prisoners, which are now held at the PRO. There are two main types: the criminal registers and the printed calendars of prisoners. The criminal registers are arranged alphabetically by county. They show all persons charged with indictable offences and give the date and result of the trial, sentence in the case of conviction, and date of execution for those convicted on capital charges. The registers are in two series: HO 26 and HO 27. A name index to HO 27 has been published by Family History Indexes.

Printed calendars of prisoners, 1868–1971, are held in record class HO 140 and also in CRIM 9 (for London, 1855–1949). Some are closed for 75 or 100 years. They list prisoners to be tried at courts of assize and quarter sessions, and provide a lot of information about them, including age and occupation, level of literacy, the name and address of the committing magistrate, details of the alleged offence, verdict and sentence. Like the criminal registers, they are in alphabetical

Criminal registers	Date range	Coverage
HO 26	1791–1806	Middlesex
	1807–11	Old Bailey only
	1812–49	Middlesex
HO 27	1805–7	England and Wales except Middlesex
	1807–11	England and Wales except Old Bailey
	1811–49	England and Wales except Middlesex
	1850–92	England and Wales

order by county. Although some of these calendars exist for earlier periods, survival is patchy; you can find some in the PRO, mainly in PCOM 2 and in various ASSI series, while others are in local record offices. Some of these early printed calendars are lists of prisoners to be tried, rather than those who have been tried, so they do not include information about verdict or sentence. Lists of those to be tried at the Old Bailey (Central Criminal Court) are in HO 16 for 1815–49 and in HO 77 for 1782–1853. The lists in HO 77 are printed and include information about the outcome of the trial.

If you know the location of a prisoner, you can trace his or her prison career via the quarterly returns in HO 24 and PCOM 8. If you know that someone was in prison between 1843 and 1871, then try PCOM 6, which indexes the court orders in PCOM 5. These not only authorize imprisonment and transfers between prisons but also give the name of the convict (and any aliases), age, marital status, trade or occupation, crime, date and place of committal and conviction, sentence, name and residence of next of kin, literacy level, religion and a physical description, together with information as to previous convictions and character.

A 'ticket of leave' enabled convicts to be released early on licence, subject to good behaviour. Registers of licences issued between 1853 and 1887 are in PCOM 3 (for men) and PCOM 4 (for women). They are listed by number, so use the indexes in PCOM 6 to trace them. The indexes cover 1853–81 for men and 1853–85 for women. The licences will tell you about appearance, age, marital status, educational level, occupation, previous convictions, conduct while in prison, name and address of next of kin, religion and health. They are also annotated with details of any offence or misbehaviour after release.

If you are still stuck, try the registers of habitual criminals. These were compiled by local prisons and recorded name and alias, age, description, trade, prison from which released, date of liberation, offence, sentence, term of supervision, intended residence, distinguishing marks and any previous convictions, together with a photograph. These local registers formed the basis of an alphabetical national register of habitual criminals, some of which survive. The PRO has some of these national registers (which do not include photographs) in PCOM 2/404 (1869–76) and in MEPO 6/1–52 (1881–2, 1889–1940); they are closed for 75 years from the date of creation. Others may survive at local record offices. The PRO also has the local prison registers of habitual criminals for Birmingham, 1871–5 (PCOM 2/296–299, 430–434); and Cambridge, 1875–7 (PCOM 2/300). Other local registers are believed to be still in the custody of the relevant prisons and police services.

You might also find it useful to look at the surviving registers of habitual drunkards, 1903–14 (MEPO 6/77–88).

Are there any prison registers?

Once you have discovered the name of the prison in which your ancestor was detained, you will naturally want to find a prison register. This may be difficult: there was no systematic policy on the collection or retention of prison registers. They are worth looking for, but the information given in prison registers is variable. In general, you are likely to find a description of the prisoner (sometimes with a photograph), together with details of occupation, marital status, aliases and previous character. They may also give an indication of discharge or transfer to another prison. The PRO does have various registers, mainly for the 19th century. These include the prison ships or 'hulks' that were moored in British coastal waters (Woolwich, Chatham, Sheerness, Portsmouth and Plymouth) to house prisoners (usually, but not always, those awaiting transportation) for the period 1776–1857. There are also some records of the hulks moored in Gibraltar and Bermuda until 1875.

You should also look at the lists of prisoners that were compiled quarterly for return to the Home Office. These contain lots of brief but interesting extra details such as assessments of behaviour, state of health, transfers to other gaols and date of release.

In future, prison registers will be deposited in local record offices; and prison registers created after 1878 are now more likely to be found in either a local record office or the prison concerned than at the PRO. Since some of the earlier 19th-century registers are already in local record offices, the PRO is undertaking a study on the relationship between its holdings of prisons records and those in local record offices. A final decision on the future location of the records will be taken once the study is complete. It is all too easy to waste time by going to the wrong record office – so check before you go. Hawkings, *Criminal Ancestors* has a useful (but now dated) list of prison registers held in local record offices.

Prison registers in the PRO	Coverage
PCOM 2	1770–1951 (prisons and hulks)
HO 9	1802–49 (hulks)
HO 23	1838–75
HO 24	1838–75
KB 32/33	1826 (Millbank only)
Quarterly returns in the PRO	
HO 8	1824–76 (prisons and hulks)
T 38	1802–31 (hulks)
ADM 6	1819–34 (*Cumberland* and *Dolphin* only)
HO 7/3	1823–8 (*Antelope, Coromandel, Dromedary* and *Weymouth* only)
T 1	Includes some registers and returns of prisoners in the hulks, but they are difficult to find because they are so poorly catalogued.

CAPITAL PUNISHMENT AND TRANSPORTATION

At the beginning of the 19th century there were over 300 capital offences. Many people were sentenced to death for offences that we would now regard as trivial, although in reality it was unusual for more than about 10 per cent of the sentences to be carried out. The purpose of the death penalty was to provide a theatrical reinforcement of social values – not to create mass revulsion.

There were several ways in which individuals were saved from death. Two were controlled by the trial jury. The first was 'pious perjury'. As explained above, the value of goods stolen was often crucial to the definition of the charge. In bringing in its verdict, the jury had to declare both that the offender was guilty of the theft and the value of the goods stolen. To save a defendant from the gallows, all the jury had to do was to undervalue the goods. This might lead to obvious absurdities, such as valuing a gold sovereign at less than 12 (old) pence. The second method was returning a 'partial verdict'. This involved the jury declaring that something essential to the legal definition of the charge was absent; for example, a charge of housebreaking or burglary could be transformed into a lesser crime by declaring the defendant guilty of theft but not of breaking and entering.

Another safeguard was 'benefit of clergy'. This started out as a way of ensuring that clergymen would be tried by their own church courts. In medieval times, the easiest way to prove that someone was a clergyman was to establish that he was educated – so the test for benefit of clergy soon turned into a test of literacy. The literacy test was abolished in 1706, but long before then the scope had gradually widened. It was granted to men who were illiterate, and during the 17th century it was even extended to women. Not unnaturally some people regarded this as an abuse of the system, so there were also moves to restrain its use. Benefit of clergy was removed from some offences; and where it remained, it was restricted to first offenders – who were supposed to be branded on the hand so that they would not be able to claim twice.

A seemingly more attractive option was provided by transportation, which removed criminals from society without actually killing them. Transportation was cheap. It also took people away from criminal haunts and associates and promised them a new life in a new world, at the same time creating a supply of labour for the developing colonies. Transportation was used from 1615 as a condition of reprieve, and in 1718 became a sentence in its own right. Until 1776 convicts were sent to the American colonies. The American Revolution stopped the flow of prisoners across the Atlantic and led to increasing overcrowding in the prisons. A supposedly temporary solution was to provide extra accommodation in old ships – the 'hulks' (see p. 36). Transportation resumed in 1787, when the first fleet sailed for Australia. At its peak, in the 1830s, it is estimated that some 4,000 individuals were being sent to Australia annually.

The royal power of mercy also saved convicts both from the gallows and from transportation. Sometimes, as he passed sentence, the judge would announce that he intended to recommend a pardon. Or the criminal, perhaps together with his/her friends and relatives, would petition the crown for a pardon. A pardon usually involved reducing a death sentence to transportation, or transportation to imprisonment. In times of war, the sentence might be commuted on condition of enlistment in the armed forces.

The petitions could generate a mass of supporting documentation (see pp. 41–2), including letters, character references, and reports from the judge. Sometimes they backfired and generated a similar campaign to *prevent* a pardon. Not unnaturally, applications were more likely to succeed when they came from those who had influential friends or supporters and/or were able to establish mitigating factors, such as youth (or, conversely, extreme age) or provocation, and who could also provide evidence of previous good character. Applications for mercy (see p. 41) provide a treasure trove of information for family and social history. For an overview of their use and contents, see Carter, 'Early Nineteenth-century Criminal Petitions'.

From the early 19th century it was accepted that the criminal justice system should be made more rational. There was also a growing belief that it was possible to reform people by effective prison regimes. Accordingly, the number of crimes that attracted the death penalty was systematically reduced. Transportation was effectively ended in 1857, although it was not finally abolished until 1867. Imprisonment came to be a sentence in its own right, the death penalty being reserved for particularly atrocious offences such as treason and murder. Even then, there was still a chance that the Home Secretary might commute the sentence to imprisonment. The death penalty was abolished in 1956.

RECORDS OF SENTENCES, PARDONS AND APPEALS FOR MERCY

Details of sentences are usually noted on the indictment. Look at the annotations carefully – they may show you a partial verdict, pious perjury or benefit of clergy in action. Gaol books sometimes have similar annotations. Remember that, as with all legal records, the annotations are usually entered *above* rather than below the entry to which they relate.

For those who were transported, you have several possible lines of research. There are a number of published works and indexes (see p. 11). The sources listed above for imprisonment can be used for transportees too, and applications for mercy will provide quality evidence about your ancestor's life. The transportation registers in HO 11 will tell you where and when a convict was tried. These are not listed by the convict's name, but by the ship and date of departure, so you will need to have one of these items of information to narrow your search.

Transportees to Australia

Many documents about convicts transported to Australia have been microfilmed by the Australian Joint Copying Project and are available at the National Library in Canberra and at the Mitchell Library in Sydney.

Applications for mercy are most likely to be held in the PRO, but don't neglect the possibility of finding petitions and correspondence elsewhere, especially among the papers of friends and relatives and the local rich and powerful. You may even find relevant material among the papers of the person or organization responsible for the prosecution, or of government ministers (especially those of the Home Secretary or his equivalent in earlier years).

National Register of Archives

To find out if the papers of individuals or organizations survive, and where they are held, use the National Register of Archives (NRA) database, available at the offices of the Historical Manuscripts Commission or via the internet (see p. 46). There is a dedicated terminal for consulting the NRA at the PRO.

Material about pardons and applications for mercy is scattered among the correspondence of the secretaries of state and subsequently the Home Secretary in the PRO's SP and HO series. For the content of the relevant series of records and published calendars, see under Records of Investigation and Prosecution (pp. 16–17). Specialist series start in 1784 with the judges' reports in HO 47. These provide exceptionally high-quality information, sometimes including the judge's own trial notes, which might include a virtual transcript of the trial evidence. If you are lucky, the judge will have added his own comments about the witnesses and how truthful they were, and may perhaps give his opinion of the credulity of the jurors. You may even find character references (both for and against the convict) and other personal information. Further information from trial judges, 1816–40, is filed in HO 6. It is likely to include recommendations for mercy (or otherwise!) as well as useful supporting information about the convict and his/her crime.

Petitions for mercy are held at the PRO in record series HO 17 (1819–40) and HO 18 (1839–54). They are filed in coded bundles, so you will need to start with the registers in HO 19, which list the petitions by the date they were received in the Home Office. These give the convict's name, offence and date and place of trial, plus the code number of the bundle in which the petition was filed; they often also give the result of the application. Note down the code number and then use this to identify the ordering reference for HO 17 or HO 18. A modern series of name indexes is being produced by Chambers. The registers start in 1797, so some of them contain information about petitions that no longer exist.

Major sources for pardon applications	Date coverage
HO 47	1784–1829
HO 6	1816–40
HO 17	1819–40
HO 18	1839–54
HO 188	1887–1960

There are also petitions in HO 44, HO 48, HO 49, HO 54, HO 56, but they are difficult to use because they are listed so badly. There are registers of remissions and pardons, 1887–1960, in HO 188; these give brief details of the cases, together with reasons for each decision, and each volume has its own rough index. More formal records of pardons and reprieves are in HO 13 (1782–1849) and HO 15 (1850–71).

You should also look at Home Office General Correspondence in HO 42 (1782–1820) and use the registers in HO 14 to trace papers in HO 12 (Home Office Criminal Papers Old Series, 1849–71). Similar papers after 1871 are in HO 45 and HO 144.

APPEALS

Until the creation of the appeal court in 1907, there was no right of appeal. The only review available was through the pardon process. Even though granting a pardon did not amount to an acknowledgement of any miscarriage of justice, applications for clemency did sometimes rely on claims of innocence and occasionally included new evidence or a reconsideration of evidence presented at the original trial. Even after 1907, the court of appeal had very limited powers of review. Case papers and registers are in PRO series J 81 and J 82, but these are rarely very informative. Look instead for a printed account of the case.

EXECUTIONS

There are some additional series of records relating specifically to the hanged, mainly in HO 163 (1899–1921), MEPO 3 and PCOM 9. HO 336 contains the complete records of nine condemned prisoners in order to illustrate the kind of information that was kept on such individuals. There is no comprehensive list, either of those executed or of the men who executed them, but HO 334/1 contains a register of prison burials (1834–1969), which provides the basis for establishing a list of the executed.

PLANNING A VISIT TO A RECORD OFFICE

1. Don't waste time by going to the wrong archive. Check that it holds the records you need!

2. Check opening hours and facilities. You will find PRO opening hours on the PRO's website.

3. If you plan to use a laptop, check availability of sockets.

4. Take pencils and a notebook with you. Record offices don't allow pens in their searchrooms, and some (including the PRO) limit the number of loose sheets of paper you can take in.

5. Find out about lockers – you won't be able to take bags into the searchroom. For a locker at the PRO, you will need a £1 coin (which is returnable).

6. Plan a search strategy before you go. Don't try to do too much in one day – and be prepared to make a return visit, if necessary.

SELECT LIST OF INTERNET RESOURCES

A2A
(Access to Archives)
accessible via Public Record Office website

British Library Newspaper Library
www.bl.uk

Cyndi's List
(for prisons, prisoners and outlaws)
www.cyndislist.com/prisons.htm

Federation of Family History Societies (FFHS)
www.ffhs.org.uk

Genealogical Society of Utah
(includes details of LDS Family History Centres)
www.familysearch.com

GENUKI
(for links to UK family-history sources)
www.genuki.org.uk

Historical Manuscripts Commission
www.hmc.gov.uk

National Archives of Ireland
(transportation records database)
www.nationalarchives.ie/search01.html

National Register of Archives
accessible via Historical Manuscripts Commission website

Public Record Office
www.pro.gov.uk

Rootsweb
(includes discussion list for convict ancestry)
www.rootsweb.com

Lincolnshire convicts (1788–1840)
www.demon.co.uk/lincs-archives/convicts.htm

Port Arthur historic site
www.portarthur.org.au

Society of Genealogists (SoG)
www.sog.org.uk

USEFUL ADDRESSES

▶ **British Library Newspaper Library**
Colindale Avenue
London NW9 5HE
Telephone: 020 7412 7353

▶ **Corporation of London Record Office**
PO Box 270
Guildhall
Aldermanbury
London EC2P 2EJ
Telephone: 020 7332 1251

▶ **Federation of Family History Societies**
Administrator
PO Box 2425
Coventry CV5 6YX

▶ **Genealogical Society of Utah**
British Isles Family History Service Center
185 Penns Lane
Sutton Coldfield
West Midlands B76 8JU

▶ **Guildhall Library**
Aldermanbury
London EC2P 2EJ
Telephone: 020 7332 1863

▼ **Historical Manuscripts Commission**
  Quality House
  Quality Court
  Chancery Lane
  London WC2A 1HP
  Telephone: 020 7242 1198

▼ **London Metropolitan Archives**
  40 Northampton Road
  London EC1R 0HB
  Telephone: 020 7332 3820

▼ **Public Record Office**
  Kew
  Richmond
  Surrey TW9 4DU
  General telephone number: 020 8876 3444
  Telephone number for enquiries and advance
  document ordering (with exact references only):
  020 8392 5200

▼ **Society of Genealogists**
  14 Charterhouse Buildings
  Goswell Road
  London EC1M 7BA
  Telephone: 020 7251 8799

ASSIZE TRIALS: RECORDS HELD BY THE PRO

County	Crown & Gaol Books	Indictments		Depositions		Other
England						
Beds	1863–76	1658–98	ASSI 16	1832–76	ASSI 36	ASSI 34
						ASSI 38
						ASSI 39
	ASSI 32					ASSI 15
Berks	1734–1863	1693–1850	ASSI 94	1876–	ASSI 13	
	1876–1945	1851–	ASSI 95			
	ASSI 33					
	ASSI 11					
	1657–1971	1650–	ASSI 5	1719–	ASSI 6	ASSI 4
	1847–1951					ASSI 9
						ASSI 10
	ASSI 2					ASSI 93
	ASSI 3					
Bucks	1863–76	1642–99	ASSI 16	1832–76	ASSI 36	ASSI 34
	1734–1863	1695–1850	ASSI 94	1876–	ASSI 13	ASSI 38
	1876–1945	1851–	ASSI 95			ASSI 39
	ASSI 32					ASSI 15
	ASSI 33					
	ASSI 11					
Cambs	1902–43	1642–99	ASSI 16	1834–	ASSI 36	ASSI 34
	1863–	1692–1850	ASSI 94			ASSI 38
	1734–1863	1851–	ASSI 95			ASSI 39
	ASSI 31					
	ASSI 32					
	ASSI 33					

County	Crown & Gaol Books		Indictments		Depositions		Other
Cheshire	1532–1831 1341–1659 1831–1938 1835–83 1945–51	CHES 21 CHES 24 ASSI 61 ASSI 62 ASSI 79	1831–1945 1945–	ASSI 64 ASSI 83	1831–1944 1945–	ASSI 65 ASSI 84	ASSI 59 ASSI 63 ASSI 66 ASSI 67
Cornwall	1730–1971 1670–1824	ASSI 21 ASSI 23	1801–	ASSI 25	1861– 1951–3	ASSI 26 ASSI 82	ASSI 24 ASSI 30
Cumberland	1714–1873 1665–1810	ASSI 41 ASSI 42	1607–1876 1877–	ASSI 44 ASSI 51	1613–1876 1877–	ASSI 45 ASSI 52	ASSI 43 ASSI 46 ASSI 47 ASSI 93
Derbys	1818–1945	ASSI 11	1868– 1662, 1667, 1687	ASSI 12 ASSI 80	1862–	ASSI 13	ASSI 15
Devon	1746–1971 1670–1824	ASSI 21 ASSI 23	1801–	ASSI 25	1861– 1951–3	ASSI 26 ASSI 82	ASSI 24 ASSI 30

County	Crown & Gaol Books		Indictments		Depositions		Other
Dorset	1746–1971 1670–1824	ASSI 21 ASSI 23	1801–	ASSI 25	1861– 1951–3	ASSI 26 ASSI 82	ASSI 24 ASSI 30
Durham	1770–1876 1753–1858 1858–1944	DURH 15 DURH 16 ASSI 41	1582–1877 1876–	DURH 17 ASSI 44	1843–76 1877–	DURH 18 ASSI 45	DURH 19 ASSI 46 ASSI 47 ASSI 93
Essex	1734–1943 1826–	ASSI 31 ASSI 32	1559–1688 1689–1850 1851–	ASSI 35 ASSI 94 ASSI 95	1825–	ASSI 36	ASSI 34 ASSI 38 ASSI 39
Glos	1657–1971 1847–1951	ASSI 2 ASSI 3	1662–	ASSI 5	1719–	ASSI 6	ASSI 4 ASSI 9 ASSI 10 ASSI 93
Hants	1746–1971 1670–1824	ASSI 21 ASSI 23	1801–	ASSI 25	1861– 1951–3	ASSI 26 ASSI 82	ASSI 24 ASSI 30
Herefordshire	1657–1971 1847–1951	ASSI 2 ASSI 3	1627–	ASSI 5	1719–	ASSI 6	ASSI 4 ASSI 9 ASSI 10 ASSI 93

County	Crown & Gaol Books		Indictments	Assizes	Depositions		Other
Herts	1734–1943 1826–	ASSI 31 ASSI 32	1573–1688 1689–1850 1851–	ASSI 35 ASSI 94 ASSI 95	1829–	ASSI 36	ASSI 34 ASSI 38 ASSI 39
Hunts	1902–43 1863– 1734–1863	ASSI 31 ASSI 32 ASSI 33	1643–98 1693–1850 1851–	ASSI 16 ASSI 94 ASSI 95	1851–	ASSI 36	ASSI 34 ASSI 38 ASSI 39
Kent	1734–1943 1826–	ASSI 31 ASSI 32	1559–1688 1689–1850 1851–	ASSI 35 ASSI 94 ASSI 95	1812–	ASSI 36	ASSI 34 ASSI 38 ASSI 39
Lancs	1524–1843 1686–1877	PL 25 PL 28	1660–1867 1877–	PL 26 ASSI 51	1663–1867 1877–	PL 27 ASSI 52	PL 28 ASSI 46 ASSI 53 ASSI 93
Leics	1818–64 1864–75 1876–1945	ASSI 11 ASSI 32 ASSI 11	1653, 1656 1864–75 1876–	ASSI 80 ASSI 35 ASSI 12	1862 1863–75 1876–	ASSI 13 ASSI 36 ASSI 13	ASSI 15 ASSI 34 ASSI 38 ASSI 39
Lincs	1818–1945	ASSI 11	1868– 1652–79	ASSI 12 ASSI 80	1862–	ASSI 13	ASSI 15

County	Crown & Gaol Books		Indictments		Depositions		Other
London & Middlesex	1834–1949	CRIM 6	1834–1957 1833–1971	CRIM 4 CRIM 5	1839– 1923–	CRIM 1 CRIM 2	CRIM 7 CRIM 8 CRIM 9 CRIM 10 CRIM 11 CRIM 12 CRIM 13
Monmouthshire	1657–1971 1847–1951	ASSI 2 ASSI 3	1666–	ASSI 5	1719–	ASSI 6	ASSI 4 ASSI 9 ASSI 10 ASSI 93
Norfolk	1902–43 1863– 1734–1863	ASSI 31 ASSI 32 ASSI 33	1606–99 1692–1850 1851–	ASSI 16 ASSI 94 ASSI 95	1817–	ASSI 36	ASSI 34 ASSI 38 ASSI 39
Northants	1818–64 1864–76 1876–1945	ASSI 11 ASSI 32 ASSI 11	1659–60 1864–75 1876–	ASSI 80 ASSI 95 ASSI 12	1862 1864–75 1876–	ASSI 13 ASSI 36 ASSI 13	ASSI 15 ASSI 34 ASSI 38 ASSI 39
Northumberland	1714–1944 1665–1810	ASSI 41 ASSI 42	1607–	ASSI 44	1613–	ASSI 45	ASSI 43 ASSI 46 ASSI 47 ASSI 93

County	Crown & Gaol Books		Indictments	Depositions	Other
Notts	1818–1945	ASSI 11	1868– 1663–4, 1682	ASSI 12 ASSI 80	1862–	ASSI 13	ASSI 15
Oxon	1657–1971 1847–1951	ASSI 2 ASSI 3	1661– 1688	ASSI 5 PRO 30/80	1719–	ASSI 6	ASSI 4 ASSI 9 ASSI 10 ASSI 93
Rutland	1818–64 1864–76 1876–1945	ASSI 11 ASSI 32 ASSI 11	1667, 1685 1864–75 1876–	ASSI 80 ASSI 95 ASSI 12	1862 1864–73 1876–	ASSI 13 ASSI 36 ASSI 13	ASSI 15 ASSI 34 ASSI 38 ASSI 39
Shropshire	1657–1971 1847–1951	ASSI 2 ASSI 3	1654–	ASSI 5	1719–	ASSI 6	ASSI 4 ASSI 9 ASSI 10 ASSI 93
Somerset	1730–1971 1670–1824	ASSI 21 ASSI 23	1801–	ASSI 25	1861– 1951–3	ASSI 26 ASSI 82	ASSI 24 ASSI 30

County	Crown & Gaol Books		Indictments		Depositions		Other
Staffs	1657–1971 1847–1951	ASSI 2 ASSI 3	1662– 1662	ASSI 5 ASSI 80	1719–	ASSI 6	ASSI 4 ASSI 9 ASSI 10 ASSI 93
Suffolk	1902–43 1863– 1734–1863	ASSI 31 ASSI 32 ASSI 33	1653–98 1689–1850 1851–	ASSI 16 ASSI 94 ASSI 95	1832–	ASSI 36	ASSI 34 ASSI 38 ASSI 39
Surrey	1734–1943 1826–	ASSI 31 ASSI 32	1559–1688 1689–1850 1851–	ASSI 35 ASSI 94 ASSI 95	1820–	ASSI 36	ASSI 34 ASSI 38 ASSI 39
Sussex	1734–1943 1826–	ASSI 31 ASSI 32	1559–1688 1689–1850 1851–	ASSI 35 ASSI 94 ASSI 95	1812–	ASSI 36	ASSI 34 ASSI 38 ASSI 39
Warks	1818–1945	ASSI 11	1868– 1652, 1688	ASSI 12 ASSI 80	1862–	ASSI 13	ASSI 15
Westmorland	1714–1873 1718–1810	ASSI 41 ASSI 42	1607–1876 1877–	ASSI 44 ASSI 51	1613–1876 1877–	ASSI 45 ASSI 52	ASSI 43 ASSI 46 ASSI 47 ASSI 53 ASSI 93

County	Crown & Gaol Books		Indictments		Depositions		Other	
Wilts	1746–1971	ASSI 21	1729	ASSI 25	1861–	ASSI 26	ASSI 24	
	1670–1824	ASSI 23	1801–		1951–3	ASSI 82	ASSI 30	
Worcs	1657–1971	ASSI 2	1662–	ASSI 5	1719–	ASSI 6	ASSI 4	
	1847–1951	ASSI 3					ASSI 9	
							ASSI 10	
							ASSI 93	
Yorks	1718–1863	ASSI 41	1607–1863	ASSI 44	1613–1863	ASSI 45	ASSI 15	
	1658–1811	ASSI 42	1864–76	ASSI 12	1868–76	ASSI 13	ASSI 43	
	1864–76	ASSI 11	1877–	ASSI 51	1877–	ASSI 52	ASSI 46	
							ASSI 47	
							ASSI 53	
							ASSI 93	
Wales								
Anglesey	1831–1938	ASSI 61	1831–1945	ASSI 64	1831–1944	ASSI 65	ASSI 59	
	1835–83	ASSI 62	1945–	ASSI 83	1945–	ASSI 84	ASSI 63	
	1945–51	ASSI 79					ASSI 66	
							ASSI 67	

County	Crown & Gaol Books		Indictments		Depositions		Other
Breconshire	1841–2 1844–1946 1945–51	ASSI 74 ASSI 76 ASSI 79	1834–1945 1945–	ASSI 71 ASSI 83	1837– 1945–	ASSI 72 ASSI 84	ASSI 73 ASSI 77
Caernarvon- shire	1831–1938 1835–83 1945–51	ASSI 61 ASSI 62 ASSI 79	1831–1945 1945–	ASSI 64 ASSI 83	1831–1944 1945–	ASSI 65 ASSI 84	ASSI 59 ASSI 63 ASSI 66 ASSI 67
Cardiganshire	1841–2 1844–1946 1945–51	ASSI 74 ASSI 76 ASSI 79	1834–1945 1945–	ASSI 71 ASSI 83	1837– 1945–	ASSI 72 ASSI 84	ASSI 73 ASSI 77
Carmarthen- shire	1841–2 1844–1946 1945–51	ASSI 74 ASSI 76 ASSI 79	1834–1945 1945–	ASSI 71 ASSI 83	1837– 1945–	ASSI 72 ASSI 84	ASSI 73 ASSI 77
Denbighshire	1831–1938 1835–83 1945–51	ASSI 61 ASSI 62 ASSI 79	1831–1945 1945–	ASSI 64 ASSI 83	1831–1944 1945–	ASSI 65 ASSI 84	ASSI 59 ASSI 63 ASSI 66
Flintshire	1831–1938 1835–83 1945–51	ASSI 61 ASSI 62 ASSI 79	1831–1945 1945–	ASSI 64 ASSI 83	1831–1944 1945–	ASSI 65 ASSI 84	ASSI 59 ASSI 63 ASSI 66 ASSI 67

County	Crown & Gaol Books	Indictments	Depositions	Other
Glamorganshire	1841–2 ASSI 74 1844–1946 ASSI 76 1945–51 ASSI 79	1834–1945 ASSI 71 1945– ASSI 83	1837– ASSI 72 1945– ASSI 84	ASSI 73 ASSI 77
Merionethshire	1831–1938 ASSI 61 1835–83 ASSI 62 1945–51 ASSI 79	1831–1945 ASSI 64 1945– ASSI 83	1831–1944 ASSI 65 1945– ASSI 84	ASSI 59 ASSI 63 ASSI 66 ASSI 67
Montgomeryshire	1831–1938 ASSI 61 1835–83 ASSI 62 1945–51 ASSI 79	1831–1945 ASSI 64 1945– ASSI 83	1831–1944 ASSI 65 1945– ASSI 84	ASSI 59 ASSI 63 ASSI 66 ASSI 67
Pembrokeshire	1841–2 ASSI 74 1844–1946 ASSI 76 1945–51 ASSI 79	1834–1945 ASSI 71 1945– ASSI 83	1837– ASSI 72 1945– ASSI 84	ASSI 73 ASSI 77
Radnorshire	1841–2 ASSI 74 1844–1946 ASSI 76 1945–51 ASSI 79	1834–1945 ASSI 71 1945– ASSI 83	1837– ASSI 72 1945– ASSI 84	ASSI 73 ASSI 77

FURTHER READING

General background

J.H. Baker, 'Criminal Courts and Procedure at Common Law 1550–1800' in J.S. Cockburn (ed), *Crime in England 1660–1800* (Oxford, 1986)

J.M. Beattie, *Crime and Courts in England 1660–1800,* (Oxford, 1986)

J.M. Beattie, *The Limits of Terror: Policing and Punishment in London 1660–1750* (Oxford, 2001)

D. Hay, P. Linebaugh, et al, *Albion's Fatal Tree* (Harmondsworth, 1975)

P. King, *Crime, Justice and Discretion in England 1740–1820* (Oxford, 2000)

E.C.L. Mullins, *Texts and Calendars II: An Analytical Guide to Serial Publications 1957–1982* (RHS guides and handbooks No. 12, 1983)

Deciphering old documents

J. Barrett and D. Iredale, *Discovering Old Handwriting* (Shire, 1995)

W.S.B. Buck, *Examples of Handwriting 1550–1650* (Society of Genealogists, 1996)

E. Gooder, *Latin for Local Historians* (Longman, 2nd edn 1978)

H. Grieve, *Examples of English Handwriting 1150–1750* (Essex Record Office Publications No. 21, Chelmsford, 1954)

D. Stuart, *Latin for Local and Family Historians: A Beginner's Guide* (Phillimore, 1995)

Guides to records

F.G. Emmison and I. Gray, *County Records (Quarter Sessions, Petty Sessions, Clerk of the Peace and Lieutenancy)* (Historical Association, Help for Students of History No. 62, 2nd edn 1987)

J.S.W. Gibson, *Local Newspapers 1750–1920 . . . A Select Location List* (FFHS, 1987)

J.S.W. Gibson, *Quarter Sessions Records for Family Historians: A Select List* (FFHS, 1995)

J.S.W. Gibson, *Record Offices, How To Find Them* (FFHS, 1987)

D.T. Hawkings, *Criminal Ancestors, A Guide to Historical Criminal Records in England and Wales* (Sutton, revised edn 1996)

G. Parry, *A Guide to the Records of the Great Sessions in Wales* (NLW, 1995)

Petty sessions

R. Paley (ed), *Justice in Eighteenth-century Hackney* (London Record Society, 1991)

Jury trials

British Trials 1660–1900 (Chadwyck Healey, 1990)

P. Carter, 'Early Nineteenth-century Criminal Petitions: An Introduction for Local Historians' in *The Local Historian* 31, Aug. 2001, pp. 130–153

J. Chambers, *Criminal Petitions Index* (Machine Breakers)

J.S. Cockburn, *A History of English Assizes 1558–1714* (Cambridge, 1972)

J.S. Cockburn *et al* (eds), *Calendar of Assize Records, Home Circuit Indictments* (London, 1975–97)

Howell's *State Trials* (compiled by W.Cobbett, T.B. Howell and T.J. Howell), 33 vols (London, 1809–26)

L.A. Knafla, *Kent at Law 1602* (HMSO, 1994)

S. Tamblin, *Criminal Registers 1805–1892* (Family History Indexes)

Transportation to America

C.M. Andrews, *Guide to the Materials for American History to 1793 in the Public Record Office of Great Britain* (Washington, 1912–14)

Calendar of State Papers, Colonial, America and West Indies 1574–1738 (London, 1869–1969)

Calendar of Treasury Books 1660–1718 (London, 1904–62)

Calendar of Treasury Papers 1557–1728 (London, 1868–89)

Calendar of Treasury Books and Papers 1729–1745 (London, 1898–1903)

P.W. Coldham, *Bonded Passengers to America 1615–1775* (Baltimore, 1983)

P.W. Coldham, *The Complete Book of Emigrants in Bondage 1614–1775* (Baltimore, 1987; supplement 1992)

Journals of the Board of Trade and Plantations 1704–1782 (London, 1920–38)

W.M. Wigfield, *The Monmouth Rebels 1685* (Somerset Record Society, 1985)

Transportation to Australia

C. Bateson, *The Convict Ships 1787–1868* (Glasgow, 2nd edn 1969)

N.G. Butlin, C.W. Cromwell and K.L. Suthern, *General Return of Convicts in NSW 1837* (Sydney, 1987)

C.J. Baxter, *Muster and Lists of NSW and Norfolk Island 1800–1802* (Sydney, 1988)

C.J. Baxter, *General Musters of NSW, Norfolk Island and Van Diemen's Land 1811* (Sydney, 1987)

C.J. Baxter, *General Muster and Lands and Stock Muster of NSW 1822* (Sydney, 1988)

C.J. Baxter, *General Muster of New South Wales 1823, 1824, 1825* (Sydney, 2001)

P.G. Fidlon and R.J. Ryan (ed), *The First Fleeters* (Sydney, 1981)

Friends of the East Sussex Record Office, *East Sussex Sentences of Transportation at Quarter Sessions 1790–1854* (Lewes, 1988)

D.T. Hawkings, *Bound for Australia* (Chichester, 1987)

R. Hughes, *The Fatal Shore: A History of Transportation of Convicts to Australia 1781–1868* (London, 1987)

New South Wales Convict Indents and Ships (Genealogical Society of Victoria) CD-ROM

L.L. Robson, *The Convict Settlers of Australia* (Melbourne, 1981)

R.J. Ryan, *The Second Fleet Convicts* (Sydney, 1982)

M.R. Sainty and K.A. Johnson (ed), *New South Wales: Census . . . November 1828* (Sydney, 1980)

I. Wyatt (ed), *Transportees from Gloucester to Australia 1783–1842* (Bristol and Gloucester Archaeological Society, 1988)

PRO PUBLICATIONS

To order books or receive information about
Public Record Office publications, please send your
name and address to:

from UK (no stamp required):
**Marketing, Public Record Office,
FREEPOST SEA 7565, Richmond TW9 4BR**

from overseas (stamp required):
**Marketing, Public Record Office, Kew,
Surrey, Great Britain TW9 4DU**

Alternatively, send an email to
bookshop@pro.gov.uk
or visit the PRO's internet bookshop at
www.pro.gov.uk/bookshop/